Amy Appleyard

Print It!

15 Fun
Printing Projects
for Kids

SCHIFFER
PUBLISHING

4880 Lower Valley Road • Atglen, PA 19310

About the Author

Amy Appleyard is a graphic designer, illustrator, and dedicated crafter who loves to spark creativity. She uses her printing expertise for her own projects and as a freelance illustrator. Amy's two children constantly expand her creative capabilities.

© 2020 BlueRed Press Ltd.

Library of Congress Control Number: 2020933405

Produced by BlueRed Press Ltd, 2020
Designed by Insight Design Concepts Ltd.
Type set in Neutra Text and Grilled Cheese

ISBN: 978-0-7643-6067-1
Printed in Malaysia

Published by Schiffer Publishing, Ltd.
4880 Lower Valley Road
Atglen, PA 19310
Phone: (610) 593-1777; Fax: (610) 593-2002
Email: Info@schifferbooks.com
Web: www.schifferbooks.com

For our complete selection of fine books on this and related subjects, please visit our website at www.schifferbooks.com. You may also write for a free catalog.

Schiffer Publishing's titles are available at special discounts for bulk purchases for sales promotions or premiums. Special editions, including personalized covers, corporate imprints, and excerpts, can be created in large quantities for special needs. For more information, contact the publisher.

We are always looking for people to write books on new and related subjects. If you have an idea for a book, please contact us at proposals@schifferbooks.com.

Contents

Introduction

Printed things are all around us. Most of this printing is done by machines: the printing on fabrics, clothes, and packaging, newspapers and cards—even this book. Printing lets you make lots of copies of your designs, but unlike using a machine, each print *you* create will be unique and completely your own. Your prints will change depending on how hard you press down (pressure), the color of ink you choose, where you put your design, and on what kind of surface or type of material you choose to print. This is what makes printmaking such fun!

I've created fifteen fabulous projects that will show you lots of different ways of printing, so that you can produce beautiful and useful handprinted designs. There are helpful tips to guide you along the way, and lots of ideas to help you create your own printmaking projects.

You can easily make all of the projects at home. You will need to find a few things first, though, such as plenty of paper (including paper to cover your work surface) as well as some old clothes or an oversized T-shirt or apron that you won't mind getting messy. Sometimes you'll also need a helpful adult for some parts of these projects. A few specialty printing materials are required (these can be bought from craft stores or online), but most of the materials for the projects can be found around your home—especially in the recycling bins!

I really hope you get as much enjoyment out of printing these projects as I've had creating them, and that you will be inspired to continue with your own printing projects in the future. But above all, have fun!

Opposite page:
Above: A simple way to dry printed papers.
Bottom left: Cushion printed with feathers.
Bottom right: Flying block-printed kites.

This page:
Above: Toy bags printed with interesting shapes.
Below: A crocodile printed using sticks of rhubarb cut in different directions.

Tools and Materials

Preparation

Good preparation helps prevent mess. If possible, make two separate areas—one for clean work and one for printing—even if the only space you have is at either end of a table. **Newspaper** or a **roll of paper** that can be taped down onto the table is ideal for protecting your work surfaces. **Baby wet wipes** are great to keep handy, since they can clean up everything, from the ink on your roller handle or your finger tips to stray blobs of ink on your printing block. It's also a good idea to have a bowl of warm water ready before you start printing, so if ink gets on your fingers you can easily clean them without touching anything else.

General Supplies

- **Binder clips**, a.k.a. **bulldog clips**, for hanging your prints up to dry
- **Craft glue**. I use washable PVA glue for anything that needs sticking, such as the printing blocks.
- **Cotton swabs** are handy for cleaning up small areas.
- **Cutting mat** for protecting your work surface from cuts, and as a useful aid when guides are needed, as well as a **craft knife** and a **metal safety ruler**
- **Masking tape** is used to hold items in place, for guides, or to prevent ink from printing where you don't want it.
- **Rags** or **paper towels** are helpful for mopping up spills or drying off tools in between changing ink colors. They don't need to be anything special (I use an old kitchen cloth), just able to absorb water and ink, and something that you are okay about throwing away afterward.
- **Tracing paper** or **baking parchment** and **pencil** for tracing your designs onto your printing block. **Carbon transfer paper** is also really handy, since it gives a crisp clean tracing that can be easily removed.

Acrylic Paint

Available in tubes or jars, the colors are easy to mix but dry very quickly. They can be mixed with a **slow-drying medium** to lengthen the time you can work with the paint, and make them easier to print with.

Block-Printing Inks

These are thicker than acrylic paint and have a sticky feel. They dry more slowly and are designed to be used with nonabsorbent materials such as lino. They are used mostly with a roller.

Fabric Paint

Made for printing on cloth, they need to be ironed when they are dry to fix the paint. Prints like this are permanent and will not be affected by washing. You can also use **textile-printing medium**, which is mixed 1:1 (that is, half and half) with acrylic paint.

Inks

Inks for printmaking can be oil or water based. For the projects in this book I have used only water-based inks. I prefer these because they let your prints dry much quicker than oils, and your tools can easily be cleaned in water.

Ink Pads

These come in a wide variety of colors for use on paper only, or for both fabric and paper. I prefer ones with a raised pad since these don't limit the size of the stamp you can ink.

Screen-Printing Ink

Made to flow through the thin mesh of the screen, this kind of ink is runny.

Different surfaces (from left to right):
thick drawing paper, colored paper, Japanese
straw silk paper, cotton fabric, felt, leather, and wood.

Printing Surfaces
Printing Paper

There's so much variety here that you will have plenty of choice. Paper can be handmade, or machine-made from materials such as wood pulp, cotton rag, pulped linen, bamboo, grass, or synthetic materials. There are different weights (the heavier the gsm—grams per square meter—the thicker the paper), and a range of surfaces, including smooth, textured, coated, and uncoated. It makes a big difference which paper you use. A smooth, matte paper is a good starting point for an even print. Textured papers need more ink and pressure because their surface is more uneven but can give fantastic results. Glossy and coated papers can be harder to use, since the ink often smears and smudges.

Try experimenting with different papers and see how varied your prints can look.

Fabric

The range of fabrics you can use is as vast as paper, but the same rules apply. A tightly woven, smooth fabric (such as cotton or linen) will give the best results. Textured fabric needs more ink and pressure, and slippery fabrics (such as silk and satin) can easily slip while printing, making smudges difficult to avoid. If you'll need to wash the fabric after you have printed it (a T-shirt, for example), prewash and dry it before printing on it. Washing makes the fabric dirt-free and removes any chemical treatment that could prevent the ink from soaking in. Your fabric needs to be crease-free and flat to avoid uneven printing, so iron it first. If the item you are printing on has two sides (like a T-shirt, cushion, or pencil case), make sure you put a piece of card or paper in between the layers of fabric to act as a barrier and prevent ink from seeping through.

Other Surfaces

The general rule for all printing surfaces is that they must be smooth, dirt free, and flat. So think creatively! Your next printing project could be on wood, stone, or leather.

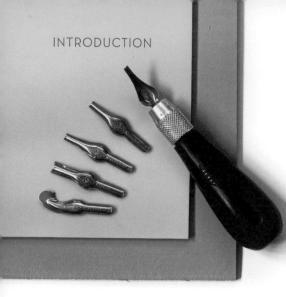

Adults should exercise sensible caution on all projects that involve sharp implements.

Lino Cutting

Lino comes in sheets or mounted on blocks. The most readily available types are **traditional lino** or alternatives such as **Essdee SoftCut** and **Easy Carve.** I recommend you try one of the last two if you can, since they have a softer and easier-to-work surface. Traditional lino is much tougher and best worked slightly warm. You can do this by sitting on it, using a hair dryer, or placing it on top of a radiator for a few minutes—or putting it out in the sunshine.

Lino Cutters

There are a variety of blades available for making different-shaped cuts, from fine detail to removing large sections. These can be bought as individual tools or as a handle with removable blades. The interchangeable blades are fitted into the handle and secured in place by twisting the clamping ring to fix the blade in position. They are very sharp.

Screen Printing

Screen printing involves a frame stretched with fine fabric. Ink is forced through the fine holes of the fabric mesh, using a rubber **squeegee**. Your design is transferred to the front of the screen with **drawing fluid** and a **paintbrush.** The areas that you don't want to print are blocked out with **screen block** or a stencil. **Screen-printing tape** or **packing tape** is used to mask the sides of the frame. A **damp cloth** and **misting bottle** are also useful.

Rollers

I use two. I keep one for inking and the other for smoothing the paper or fabric over the printed surface to create my print. This means that I will always have one clean roller, and reduces the risk of transferring ink onto the back of my print. An alternative to your second roller could be a **baren** (Japanese wooden printing tool) or, more simply, the back of a large **wooden spoon** or a small **rolling pin.**

Bench Hook

A bench hook is helpful if you are new to carving. It is a wooden board that hooks over your table edge and provides a solid base for cutting. It holds your block steady and prevents it from slipping.

Drypoint

Drypoint is a simple form of engraving that involves cutting into a plate. You will need an **etching needle** or sharp tool such as an **awl,** to draw onto the plate; a light gauze cloth such as **scrim**, **muslin**, or **medical gauze**; and **cotton swabs** to remove ink from the plate's surface.

Stencils and Masks

These are barriers that stop ink from transferring onto areas of your printing surface that you don't want inked. **Stencil board** and **vinyl** are both water resistant and ensure that designs stay sharp. Paper can be used but isn't as durable. **Masking tape** and **scrap paper** can also be used for masking.

Printing Techniques

Transferring Your Design

Your printing block needs to be a mirror image of your final print. So, copy your design onto tracing paper or baking parchment. Turn the paper over and place it on top of your block so that the pencil marks are facedown. It's a good idea to use a piece of masking tape to keep it in place. Using your pencil, trace over the back of your design so that the pencil marks are transferred onto the block.

Carving Techniques

Carving tools are sharp and can easily slip, so get an adult to help you. *Always cut away* from your body, while keeping your fingers away from the blades. Keep the blade angle shallow to avoid digging too deeply into your block. Rotate the block as you carve so that you always cut away from yourself and your design, and take it slowly, since this way you stay in control and are less likely to make a mistake. You can always take more away, adding more cuts and detail. Start with your smallest blade, cutting a key line around the design. Then use your largest blade to remove the larger areas that you don't wish to print. Regularly check your design by lightly inking it with your ink pad. This will show you if any areas still need to be removed. This is now your printing plate.

Inking

Squeeze a small amount of printing ink onto the top of your printing tray (or a hard, flat surface—such as an acrylic sheet), pick a little up with your roller, and roll this out across the tray. Spread the ink out until it looks thin and even (like fine sandpaper); it should make a subtle hissing sound and feel a bit tacky. These signs tell you that the ink has coated the roller evenly, and you're ready to start printing. Place your printing block on a sheet of newspaper—or if it's a small block, hold it by the edges with your fingertips—and work the inked roller a number of times over your printing block. Roll from different directions and make sure every bit is coated with ink, rotating the block as necessary and recoating the roller as needed. When you've finished, turn the roller upside down, to prevent the inked roller from sitting in the ink or touching your work surface.

Registration and Alignment

Printing in exactly the same position every time requires accuracy. Using registration helps you keep your paper or printing blocks/plates in the same position for every print you make. Gaining confidence with this will help you achieve consistency with your printing, aid the printing of patterns, and help you achieve designs in more than one color.

Basic:

Horizontal and vertical guidelines on your printing surface help you keep your prints aligned. Line up your inked plate against these guides where they cross. Keep the lines faint so they can easily be removed (or won't show) once your ink has dried.

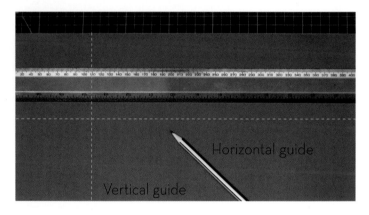

Horizontal guide

Vertical guide

Printing More than One Color

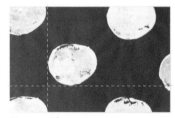

First color

Overprinted

Ensure that your ink has fully dried before overprinting. This avoids any ink from becoming smudged. Use the same guidelines as your first color to align your printing block (in this example a carved potato) in the same position to print directly over the top of your first color.

Advanced:

Creating a template, like the one opposite, will help you keep each sheet of paper you print on and your printing plate/block in the same position every time, helping to achieve consistent printing. Aligning two or more printing plates without a template can be tricky, so it is worth making in order to create successful prints.

1 Tape the top edge of a sheet of blank paper and a sheet of tracing paper to a board or a stiff sheet of cardboard so they can be lifted up.

2 Ensure that your printing paper has all been cut to the same size.

3 Place your inked printing plate underneath the sheet of tracing paper and mark its position on the paper. (You can do this by marking all four sides

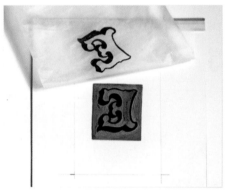

of the printing paper or just the corners). Lay the tracing paper over your inked plate and transfer your design onto the underside of the tracing paper. Allow the ink to dry (unless printing in more than one color) to avoid ink getting on your printing paper.

4 By laying your printing paper underneath the dry tracing paper you can now see where to position your paper and mark its position. Use the guides you've created to line up each sheet of your printing paper and your printing plate to ensure they are in the same position each time you print.

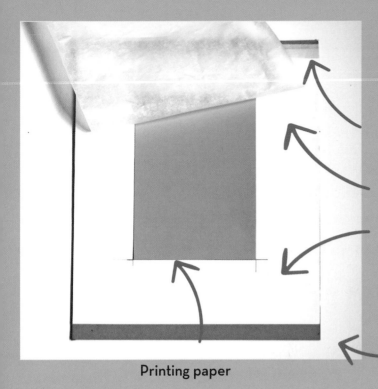

Printing paper

Printing Template

Masking tape fixes the top edge of the tracing paper and paper to your board.

Tracing paper or **baking parchment**

Sheet of **paper** to mark your guides and notes on. **Guides** show you where your printing paper and your printing plate should be positioned each time you print.

Stiff cardboard or **board**

Printing More than One Color

5 As you did in step 3, ink up your first plate, place it in position using your guides, and transfer a print onto the tracing paper.

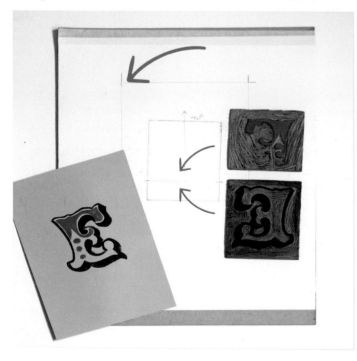

You should now have the guidelines you need to align your printing paper and each printing plate.

6 While the ink is wet, lay your second uncarved plate underneath the tracing paper and mark its position. (Adding notes or color coding your guides will help you remember which plate should go where.) Lay the tracing paper over the plate and transfer the wet ink onto its surface. Once the ink has dried on your plate, you can drawn on the design for your second color and carve it out. The transfered print acts as a guide to help you keep your two colors aligned.

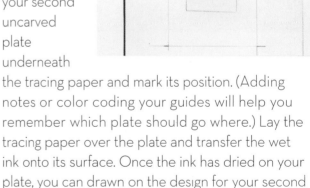

7 The template you have now created allows you to position each of your plates and your printing paper back in the same place every time you print.

Screen Printing

Tape the edges of the frame and any areas where you don't require ink. This helps to prevent the ink from seeping around the edge of your screen or onto your design, creating unwanted marks or a frame around your print. A waterproof tape such as **screen printing tape** or **packing tape** is suitable for this. It is also helpful to position your design toward the bottom of the frame, in order to mask a larger space at the top of the screen for you to spread out the ink.

Your first pull across the screen will force the ink into the frame's fabric (and secures your stencil in place if this is the technique you are using). Your subsequent pull(s) transfers the image onto your printing surface. You may find that you have to pull the ink across the screen a few times in order to achieve a good ink coverage. Pull the ink in just one direction across the screen, rather than both up and down. In order to recycle the ink at the end of your pull, angle your **squeegee** towards you, against the bottom of the frame, to scoop the remaining ink up off the screen and on to the blade. Lift the ink off the screen and return it to the top.

When you have completed your print it can help to hold down your paper as you lift up the screen, since it can sometimes stick to the wet screen.

Angle your squeegee to the screen (between 45°-60°).

Mask a larger area at the top of your screen so that the ink can be spread out without affecting your print.

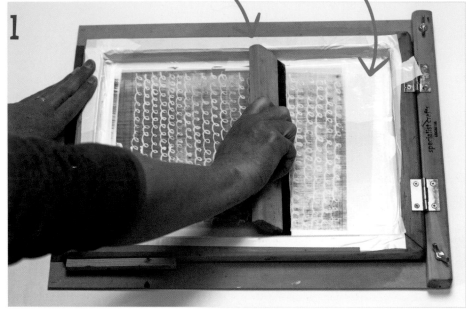

Pull your ink in one direction across the screen.

2 Turn the squeegee blade toward you in order to scoop up the remaining ink from the bottom of the screen. Lift the squeegee up off the screen and return the ink to the top to pull across the screen again.

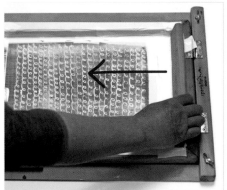

3 Repeat pulling the ink from the top, to the bottom of the screen, until you have achieved the desired ink coverage for your print.

Applying Pressure

A few test prints before printing directly on to your final surface will help you understand how much pressure you should be applying, as it is not the same for all printing techniques. Too little pressure and your print will look faded since it hasn't picked up enough ink, while too much pressure means fine detail can be lost as the ink starts to fill in. For delicate objects like fruit and flowers you will need to exert enough pressure to leave a print but not be so heavy handed that you squash them. For lino printing you will need to exert firm pressure with a **clean roller** or **baren** to ensure that your print picks up enough ink to reveal details. For drypoint printing you will first need to establish which thickness setting your pasta machine should be set on, so that your print can run through the machine with ease while also transferring enough ink onto the paper for a clear print.

A wooden spoon or a small rolling pin are good alternatives to a baren.

Troubleshooting

Imperfections are part of the charm of printmaking. If your print is not as you'd hoped here are some tips to help:

Purrfect!
Print is even, details are clear. The right amount of ink and printing pressure.

Print looks pale or patchy—not enough ink or printing pressure.

Small patches—debris left on paper or printing block.

Lines and marks outside your design—blocks need to be cleaned. If carving, cut away the marks, and if screen printing add additional masking.

Fine lines are filled in and details are lost—too much ink.

Smudged, blurred, or double image—caused by paper or block movement.

Patchy—not enough or uneven pressure has been applied. Also check that there are no imperfections (dents, debris, or dried ink) on your roller, paper, or printing block.

Colors not lining up—registration is out of alignment. To overcome this you will need to adjust your guides to compensate.

Registration

Making a perfect print every time can be tricky when you are using different layers. By using registration marks you will keep your paper and blocks in the same position for every print you make.

1 Tape a sheet of paper to a board or a stiff sheet of cardboard. Cut all your printing paper to the size you're going to use. Lay a sheet in the center, and using a pencil, mark the paper's edges and corners onto the undersheet. You will use these marks to position your paper in the exact same place *every time* you print.

2 In order to line up your second or more colors, tape a sheet of tracing paper on top of your sheet of paper.

3 Place your inked printing plate between the tracing paper and sheet of paper and mark its position on the back sheet. (Adding notes or color coding your guides will help you to remember what goes where). Lay the tracing paper over the inked plate and transfer your design onto the tracing paper.

4 While the ink is still wet, lay your second *uncarved* plate onto the back sheet and mark its position. Transfer the inked tracing paper onto the plate. When your plate is dry, add your design. This transfered print is your guide to help you keep your design aligned. Carve your second plate.

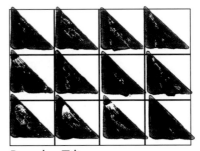

Regular Tiling:
Each tile lines up with the one next to it.

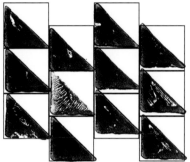

Half Drop:
Every other column is printed half a tile depth lower.

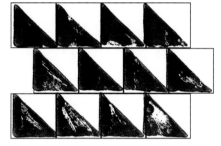

Brick repeat:
Tiles repeat like the bricks of a house, with each alternate row printed half a tile width to the right.

Rotation:
Tiles are evenly rotated around the central point.

5 The template that you have now made allows you to position your printing plates and paper back in exactly the same place every time you print. This preparation will help to make sure that your colors exactly line up.

Applying Pressure

Too little pressure and your print will look faded as it will not pick up enough ink, but too much pressure means fine detail can be lost as the ink starts to fill in the spaces. For delicate objects like fruit and flowers you will need to exert enough pressure to leave a print, but not be so heavy handed that you squash them. For lino printing you will need to go over your print with a **clean roller** or **baren** to make sure that your print is picking up enough ink to reveal the detail.

Screen Printing

Your stencil is fixed to the outside of the screen when screen printing. As you place the screen down for inking your design, it should look as you want to print it. It's important to tape over all the areas where you don't require ink.

Before printing, dampen the screen with a **damp cloth,** or **misting bottle**, to help stop the ink from thickening. Lay your screen down over the printing surface. Apply a line of ink to the top of the inside of the screen frame, and using a **squeegee** pull the ink across the screen from one end to the other, using even pressure and speed. Your first pull across the screen will force the ink into the frame's fabric (and secure your stencil in place if this is the technique you are using). Your following pulls will transfer the image onto your surface.

1. Fruit and Vegetable Printing

Bugs and Beasts

These creatures, made from printing with fruit and vegetables, not only give you an good excuse to play with your food but are a brilliant way to explore different textures and shapes. Fruit and vegetables can be cut in a number of different ways, providing lots of interesting possibilities.

Choose firm fruit and vegetables that will hold their shape when squashed during the printing process. Use their shapes and textures to form the look and character of your creatures. Try to use all the different parts of the fruit and vegetables. The leaves, stalks, roots, and fresh peelings also make interesting prints. Using a cutting board and kitchen knife, cut your fruit or vegetable in different directions—along its length, crossways, and along the diagonal. This way you'll get different textures and shapes.

Materials
Selection of firm fruit and vegetables

Acrylic paint or block-printing ink
Black pen
Cutting board
Fork or toothpicks
Kitchen knife
Paper towel
Paper
Printing tray or flat surface for mixing your paint
Roller or paintbrush
Vegetable peeler or apple corer

Flowers: I've printed the purple flower with half a brussel sprout, and the blue with mini corn. I've used chives to print the flower stalks.

16

Spring Onion Dragonfly

Spring Onion Dragonfly

Spring Onion Dragonfly

Cut off the root end to create the eyes **A**. Cut the remaining onion in half lengthways **B** Keep a piece of the green outside stalk for the wing **C**. I have cut this into a wing shape by rounding off the top.

1 If your fruit or vegetables are oozing liquid, gently pat them dry on a paper towel. This will remove some of the excess juice, which would water down the paint and make it runny.

2 Mix your paint in a printing tray, then roll it out with a roller and press your fruit or vegetable slice gently into the paint, or paint its edges with a paintbrush. Try not to overload the paint—you need enough paint to make a print, but not so much that you get a blob and lose detail. Be gentle but also firm, not heavy handed. Don't try to print too much at once—fruit and vegetables break up quickly.

Leek Snail

Slice across the leek to make a shell **A**. Skewer a toothpick through the center to keep the leek together. Cut another slice in half for the body and throw away the central pieces **B**. A split-open section from the center of the leek makes the antenna **C**.

Leek Snail

Tangerine Bee

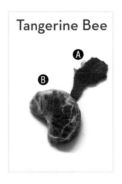

Tangerine Bee

Tangerine Bee

Wings are a strip of peel **A**. The body is a segment of tangerine **B**, first printed in yellow and then again over the top in black. You could add the black stripes with the end of the segment or a pen once your paint has dried.

Apple Butterfly

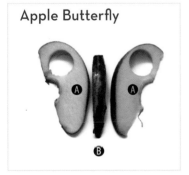

Apple Butterfly

Apple Butterfly

Cut the apple in half from top to bottom. Remove a slice and cut it in half for the wings **A**. Use an apple corer to remove a circle at the top of each wing. A thin slice of apple is used to print the body **B**. This can also be used on its edge, or trimmed down in size, for the antenna.

Tip

A fork, sweet-corn skewer, or toothpick stabbed into your fruit or vegetable makes a useful handle.

3 Try cutting areas away. The butterfly wings **A** on page 16 are made by using an apple corer to remove a circle at the top. The tail of the tiger **E** is cut from a round piece of carrot, and the leg **D** is shaped from a long section of carrot.

Carrot Tiger

Carrot Tiger

Use orange paint to print the head **A**, body **B C**, legs **D**, tail **E**, and ears **F**. Allow to dry. Print the tiger's nose stripe in white, using a long triangle **G**, and the squat triangle for a nose in black directly underneath. A thin slice of a circle of carrot creates the tiger's markings **H**, and a thinner strip can be used to make the claws and facial markings, or you can add them with a pen once they're dry. I've used **C** again, in green, to make the bushes.

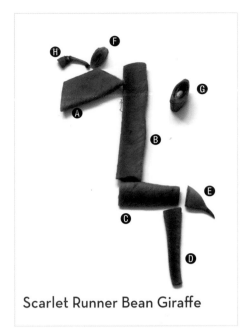

Scarlet Runner Bean Giraffe

Scarlet Runner Bean Giraffe
Use yellow to print the head **A** (remove a strip from the nose end for the ear **F**), neck **B**, and body **C** (print two, one above the another to achieve a good width). Print the top of the legs **D**, then rotate 180° and print the bottom of the leg and foot—the thicker end for the feet—tail **E**, and ear **F**. Allow to dry. Mix a brown paint and, using a slice across the bean **G**, print the giraffe's markings and tail end (this piece is also used for the flies). Use the stalk for the ossicone **H** (the hornlike structure on the head).

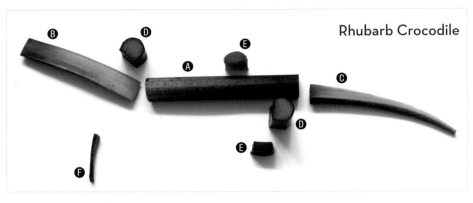

Rhubarb Crocodile

Rhubarb Crocodile
Cut a rhubarb stick in half. Keep one section for the body **A** (print two of these, one above the other to achieve a good width for the body); the other is halved again lengthways. One slice will make the jaws **B**. Cut the other at an angle for the tail **C** (I also printed this twice to make the tail fatter). An end-on slice of rhubarb makes the eye, nose, and legs **D**; smaller sections, the scales and feet **E**. Cut a thin sliver for the teeth and claws **F**. **C** can be used again, or a shorter version, to create the grasses.

4 Once your paint has dried, you can add details like the eyes and mouth with a black pen.

5 Combine the shapes you've created to make your own collection of bugs and beasts. They don't have to be realistic, just wild!

2. Cork Stamps and Decoder Disk

This project is perfect for using up any self-adhesive craft foam scraps, but you can also make stamps with small household items such as string, buttons, and bolts. Corks are the ideal size to use as a handle, and they'll also stand upright in your storage box, making the designs easier to see. You could make a few to dress up your work, or a full set of thirty-six stamps to create your own secret messages using this colorful decoder.

Materials
36 corks

3 sheets of card, different colors
Compass
Cutting mat
Etching needle or sharp tool
Ink pads
Paper fastener
Pencil
Ruler
Self-adhesive craft foam
Small scissors
Storage box

Invent a code with your friends. You'll be able to send secret messages that only they will understand!

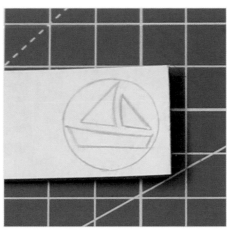

1 Use a cork as a template and draw a circle with a pencil onto the paper side of the self-adhesive craft foam.

2 Draw your design inside the circle. Keep your shapes simple, because it makes them much easier to cut out.

3 Cut out your design with a small pair of scissors. You may need the help of an adult for this part.

Tips

• Use only one color for each stamp. The color of your ink pad can easily become muddied and ruined if you mix your colors.

• If you want to add a tiny detail like a dot or an eye, first stick your foam onto the cork. You can then use the cork as a barrier for your sharp tool. Wiggle your sharp tool from side to side to make the hole bigger.

• If your stamp becomes oversaturated with ink and the details become lost, print it firmly on a paper towel a few times to absorb the excess ink.

4 On the foam side, add details with a sharp tool. The etching needle is perfect for this, but a sharp pencil works fine too.

5 Peel back the self-adhesive paper and stick it down onto the end of a cork. Continue to make thirty-five more stamps with different designs.

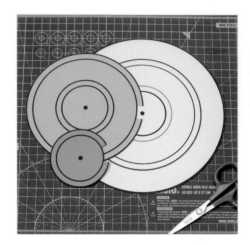

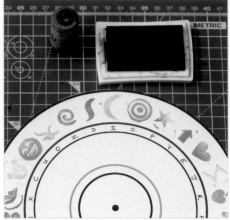

6 Copy the decoder template on page 75 onto your card with a compass and ruler. I've printed mine onto different-colored card. Cut out one of your printouts down to the red circle, and the other down to the blue. Remove one segment down to the first circle, from each of the two smaller circles. See the photo above to make sure you have the cuts in the right places.

7 Print each of your stamps into a separate segment. Add the code solution underneath (don't put this in order, since your code will be too easy to crack). I've used the largest circle for the alphabet and the middle-sized circle for numbers.

8 Use a barrier such as an eraser underneath the center of your circles, and push a pencil or compass through the center to make a hole. Push the paper fastener through the holes of all three circles and open up the back to secure the three circles together.

9 Rotate the circles to reveal the solution to each stamp. Keep your code to yourself or share with your close friends or family. If you make more than one decoder, make sure that each is exactly the same and that everyone keeps them secret!

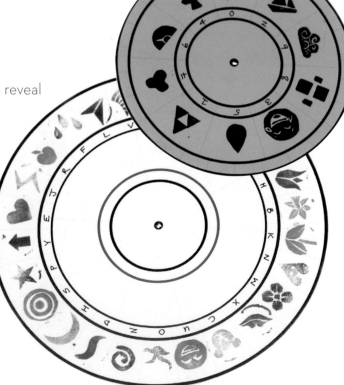

3. Drypoint with Tetra Pak®

Tetra Pak® (what many drinks cartons are made of) can be salvaged from your recycling. It's used in lots of food packaging, particularly for juice and milk cartons. Look for cardboard containers with a silver foil lining, although some packs have a white plastic lining. Both work well.

When you're printing, you will need to use a lot of pressure to squeeze the ink out of the lines you etch (cut). The flat rollers of a pasta machine are an alternative to a printing press, and it's great fun to print with. There is something exciting about seeing your print emerge from a press, even if it is a pasta machine!

You can make lots of paper money with this project—unfortunately, you can only pretend to spend it, but that's great if you create your own games or for role play.

Materials
Tetra Pak®

Block-printing ink
Cotton swab
Etching needle or sharp tool
Masking tape
Muslin cloth or rag
Newspaper
Pasta machine
Pencil
Printing paper
2 printing trays
Roller
Ruler
Scissors
2 sheets of felt cut to size
Tea towel
Tracing paper

Tips
- Don't forget that your print will be a mirror image of your etching.
- Run a couple of tests through your pasta machine to decide which setting your machine should be set on.
- Keep a bowl of warm, soapy water ready for washing your hands.

1 Wash and dry your drink containers thoroughly, then cut them open. You can use the individual panels or incorporate the folds into your design. The width of your plate must be smaller than the pasta machine rollers (my maximum width is 5.3 in. / 13.5 cm) and allow for your paper to overlap your plate (by about 3/4 in. / 2 cm).

2 Cut the paper down to size. It needs to be larger than your printing plate you made in step 1, but still able to fit through the pasta machine. Fill one of the printing trays with water and soak a couple of sheets of your already cut paper. Soaking the paper will help draw the ink out from the etched lines when you print.

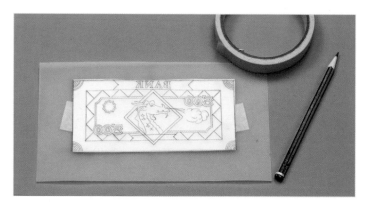

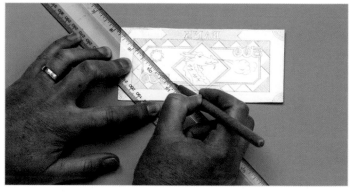

3 Transfer the template on page 74 onto the surface of your Tetra Pak® with tracing paper, a pencil, and a ruler. Hold the Tetra Pak® in place with masking tape to avoid any movement as you work.

4 With your etching needle or sharp tool, draw over your design. Add tone by adding fine lines or crosshatching; the closer together, the darker the area will be. Etch the black areas as if you were coloring in.

5 Add some ink to your second printing tray and spread it out with your roller. Ink your Tetra Pak® plate. Give it a good coating to ensure that the ink fills in all the grooves.

6 This is the messiest part! Remove the ink from the surface of the plate with your muslin cloth or rag. Use light strokes, since you don't want to pull the ink out of your etched lines.

7 A damp, not wet, cotton swab is good for cleaning areas where you want bright highlights. I've used a cotton swab to highlight the dragon's smoke, his neck and cheek, and the star.

Felt

Damp printing paper   Tetra Pak® (ink side down)

8 Wash your hands to make certain you don't transfer any ink onto your paper. Remove a sheet of printing paper from the water and lay it between a folded tea towel. Remove the excess water by patting dry. Your paper should be damp, not soaking wet. Add another sheet to soak in the water tray, ready for your next print.

9 Place your printing plate down onto your paper, and sandwich this between two sheets of felt. The felt protects your pasta machine from getting any ink on the rollers, which could ruin any further prints—or pasta making!

Flat rollers for lasagna, pasta sheets, and printing!

10 Clamp the pasta machine to your work surface, so it doesn't move. Hold your sandwich firmly together so it doesn't slip apart, and guide it through the flat rollers of the pasta machine, turning the handle until the rollers clamp your sandwich. Continue turning the handle until it has passed all the way through the machine.
Once it's dry, trim your money to size and *ta-da* … you've created your own money!

4. Monoprinting

Materials
Copy of a portrait photograph

8.5" x 11" paper
8.5" x 11" transparent acrylic
    sheet
Block-printing ink
Cotton swabs
Muslin cloth or rag
Newspaper
Printing tray
Roller
Scratch tool or paintbrush
Textures (for example, wooden
    fork, cork)

Portrait
Monoprinting allows you to be artistic and experimental at the same time! Each print can only be made once, because you work directly on the printing plate, so each print you create is unique and a total surprise. You need to work quickly, since the thin layer of ink can dry rapidly. You can work in one color or build up layers in different colors. Your results will make great personalized gifts.

Tips
- Your print will be a mirror image of your photograph, so if you want the print to be the right way around, reverse your photocopy.
- Choose a picture that isn't too busy. The image will also need to have good contrast so that you can clearly see the highlights and shadows.
- Keep a bowl of warm, soapy water ready for washing your hands.

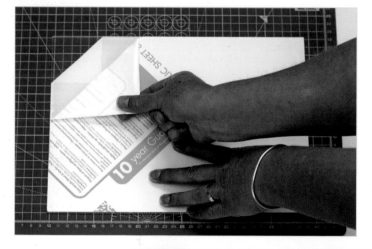

1 Choose an image and make a photocopy—take a selfie, take a photo of your pet or favorite relative, or use a picture from a magazine. Don't use an original photograph, since it will get covered in ink and ruined forever! Here I'm using a photocopy of a dog.

2 If your acrylic sheet is new, remove the film from both the back and front of the sheet before starting.

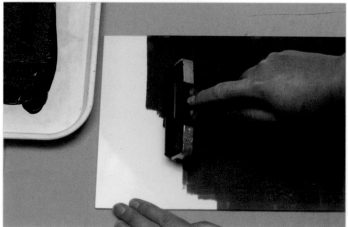

3 Lay the acrylic down on a sheet of newspaper (or scrap paper), with a white sheet of paper underneath. You don't have to do this, but it helps you see the ink on your plate. Add some ink to your printing tray and evenly coat the roller. Then use it to ink your acrylic sheet. Make sure that your sheet is totally covered with ink.

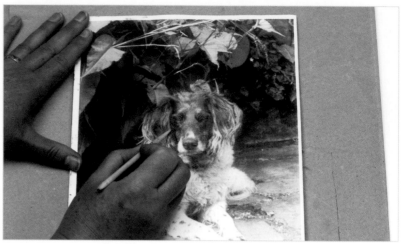

4 Sandwich a sheet of paper (your printing paper) between the inked acrylic sheet and the photocopy. Try to keep all three pieces neatly together. Always align your sheets on the top and bottom of the longest side.

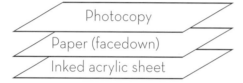

5 With a scratch tool or the end of a paintbrush, trace over the photocopy. This is where you need to work quickly, since the thin layer of ink will dry quickly. Vary the thickness and pressure of the lines you create. The scratch tool is great, since each end has a different thickness, but different ends of different-sized paintbrushes will work too. The harder you press, the darker your lines will be. Try to keep the side of your hand off the paper, since any pressure will leave a trace.

6 Add tone, or blocks of color, by rubbing your finger over the areas. Again, the harder you press, the darker your color will be.

7 You can sneak a peek at your print as you work, to make sure that you have traced everywhere. Do this by holding one corner down to keep your paper and photocopy in the same position. Don't let them slide apart even slightly!

8 Clean the plate with your rag or wash and dry it. Then add a new color to your plate. Using a rag, remove the areas where you don't want that color on your print, as outlined by the red line in my example. Lay the print back down onto the plate and add tone and detail as you did with your first color.

Add textures to your plate by making marks directly in the ink to leave an impression. You could use your rag scrunched up, scrape a cork or bottle top across the surface, or use a wooden fork or your scrape tool to draw directly on the inked plate. Don't use anything sharp for this as you need to keep your acrylic plate scratch free.

9 You can also paint directly on your plate with a paint brush and some ink. Be careful that your paint isn't too thick as it can spread when you print and move into places where you don't want it.

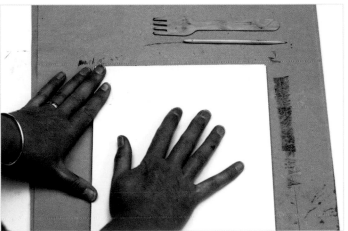

10 Place your print back down onto the printing plate (ink side down) aligning the corners. Use the palm of your hand to rub over the paper to transfer the ink. Build up layers in this way until you are happy that your print is complete.

5. Relief Printing

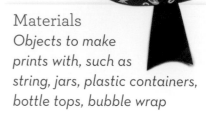

Exploring Pattern and Texture

Patterns can be made with almost anything as long as they have a flat surface. The relief is the raised part of your object that will provide you with a print, so if your object is textured, it will be the highest points that will make an impression. Bear this in mind when you are considering what things to print with, especially with the smaller objects, since these will need to be glued all at the same level to print well.

Take a good look through your recycling and around your home to see what things you can find in addition to these examples. Look out for textured items, since these can give unexpected and exciting results.

Materials
Objects to make prints with, such as string, jars, plastic containers, bottle tops, bubble wrap

Acrylic paint or block-printing ink
Cardboard
Colored paper
Craft knife
Glue brush
Metal safety ruler
Pencil and ruler
Printing tray
PVA glue
Roller or paintbrush
Scissors
Small, round, white stickers

1 Wash and dry the larger objects that you plan to print with.

2 For smaller and flimsy things (like the string and pumpkin seeds), you will need to mount them onto a stiff surface such as cardboard. Cut your cardboard down into block-sized pieces (don't make them too large). If the cardboard is thin, glue a couple of pieces together to make them firmer and more rigid.

Tips

• Ask an adult to help you with this project.
• The blade of the craft knife is very sharp, so use it with a cutting mat to protect your work surface and a metal safety ruler, keeping your fingers behind the guard when you are cutting.
• Avoid printing directly on top of any guidelines, since they will be impossible to remove later from underneath your paint.
• Don't use meat containers, even clean ones, because you could end up spreading bacteria.

Direction of pattern repeats

Salvaged plastic rope

String

Driftwood

Plastic container

Plastic container

Jar lid overprinted with spice jar base.

Bottle top

Fork head

Pumpkin seeds

3 Paint a generous layer of glue onto the cardboard, and stick down your objects. Try to keep them level with each other. Then coat the objects with a good layer of glue to make your printing block last longer. Leave your blocks to dry thoroughly before printing. This may mean leaving it overnight if your glue is very thick.

4 Evenly roll out some ink on your printing tray, and ink your printing surface. Depending on your object, you may wish to roll over it with an inked roller (for example, jar lid, plastic container), paint it with a light stoke of a paintbrush (such as string block, pumpkin seeds, fork head), or press it into the surface of the ink (for example, plastic rope/ string).

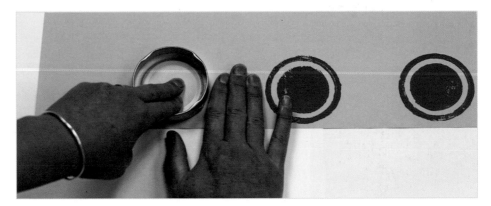

5 Make a print by pressing your inked object firmly onto the paper. You will need to recoat your object or block for every repeat you make.

Tip
Your print can still be used even if you make a mistake when printing your pattern, so don't throw it away.

6 There are a number of different ways to create a pattern. You can arrange your objects by eye, using the top of your paper as a guide; measure finger spaces between the objects as you print; use your cutting mat as a guide to measure equal spaces between your objects; or create tighter patterns by drawing horizontal and vertical guidelines with a pencil and ruler to help line up each print. But keep your marks light and print above or next to your marks, so that they can be removed once your paint has dried. The arrows next to my examples (see the diagrams on page 32) indicate how I've positioned each of my repeats to create my patterns.

7 Use your patterns to print onto fabric and larger sheets of paper or to plan printing onto an object such as a bag or cushion. Or cut your patterns up and use them in a collage, as I have for my birds.

8 Copy the shapes on page 80 for the **Bird Collage Template** onto card. Place your template onto your *dry pattern sheets* and draw around the outside of the card with a pencil and cut out the shapes.

9 Mix the cutout shapes from different sheets and stick them together with a dab of PVA glue, a glue stick, or double-sided sticky tape. For the birds eyes, I have used round, white stickers.

10 To create the clouds, use a scrunched-up scrap of bubble wrap, or similar, pressed into your rolled ink, and print the inked bubble wrap randomly across the background. Once dry, your birds can be stuck down onto the background paper.

6. Printing with Toys

Drawstring Toy Bags

Many toys make great ready-made stamps—their geometric shapes are brilliant for creating repeat patterns. Printing onto drawstring bags makes a colorful storage solution for keeping small toys tidy, from board game pieces, jigsaws, dice, and marbles to Lego® bricks, toy cars, and building blocks. They are so useful you will find yourself making them for everyone in your family!

1 Wash and dry the bags to ensure that they are clean and have no manufacturing chemicals left on them that could affect the printing. Once they're dry, iron to make them crease-free (ask an adult to help if you are not confident with ironing).

2 Insert a piece of card, covered with a sheet of newspaper that has been cut to the size of the bag, into the inside. This will prevent your paint from seeping through onto the back of the bag. The card also helps stretch the fabric and will keep it flat and crease-free (creases in the fabric will distort and spoil your printing).

Materials
Toys (for example, big and small wheels, Lego® bricks, wooden building blocks)

Cotton drawstring bags
Fabric magic pen
Fabric paint or fabric ink pads
Iron
Printing tray
Roller or paintbrush
Ruler
Scrap paper
Sheet of card and newspaper

Tips
- Before you start printing onto the bag, plan your pattern and color scheme (see pages 6 and 14 for some ideas). Printing on a sheet of similar-colored paper or a scrap piece of fabric will help you feel confident about printing onto your final surface and avoiding mistakes.
- Take the color of your fabric into consideration when choosing which color to print with. Fabric paint soaks into the fabric, so your paints will mix with the background fabric color. The rectangle on the pink bag (see right) was printed with orange paint—but when dry, it looks red.

Ironing Tips
- When ironing, don't leave the iron sitting on the fabric. Keep the iron moving across your fabric. This prevents your fabric from scalding or burning.
- Never leave your iron unattended. Switch it off.
- Once you have finished, allow the iron to cool completely before packing it away.

Wheels

3 Use your printed sample sheet to work out how the pattern layout will fit on your bag. Mark the center of the bag's width, using a fabric pen, and, with a ruler, line your pattern up with this mark; this will make certain that your design is central. The magic pen marks vanish over time. A fabric pencil or chalk that won't leave a permanent mark and can be washed out once you have fixed your printing could be used instead.

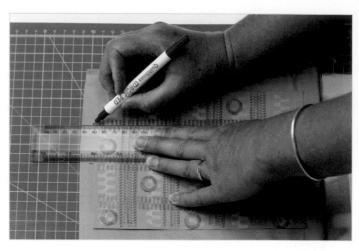

4 Mark more guides across the width and length of the bag, working from your central guide to show you where to print the wheels. The guides on a cutting mat are really helpful to ensure that your marks are truly horizontal and vertical.

5 Hold your wheel in the center, using your forefinger and thumb (the wheel should be able to rotate). Roll the wheels across your ink pad until they are well coated. (Fabric paint is also suitable to use, but I prefer the crisper detail that the ink pad provides.)

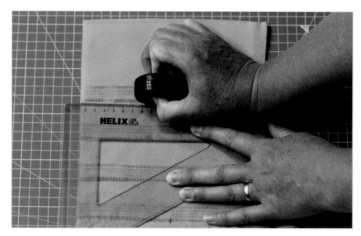

6 A straightedge can be used to guide your wheel across the bag. This will help make sure that your lines are straight. I printed the wheels in opposite directions to create a checkered pattern. Then I added the wheel, printed on its side for the circles in the alternate squares of the pattern.

7 Once dry, the ink needs to be fixed with a hot iron. Iron on a hot setting (cotton) for four to five minutes (or follow the instructions on your fabric ink pad or fabric paint bottle).

Building Blocks or Lego®

Follow instructions **1-4** for wheels. I used fabric paint for printing with the building blocks and Lego®.

> **Tip**
> If you do have a disaster, don't panic. As long as your paint is not dry or fixed, you can wash the paint from the bag and try again.

8 Mix your fabric paint in the printing tray and use a roller to roll out an even layer. Press your block into the paint. If you find the block isn't coating very well, use a paintbrush or your roller to coat the block instead.

9 Print your pattern onto your bag. I used the side of a Lego® brick, overlapping the edges to create a square, and the top of the Lego® brick for the overprinted circles.

Building-Blocks Pattern

Lego® Pattern

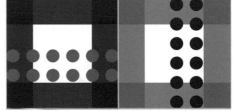

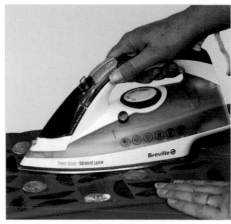

10 If you want to overprint a color, as I have with this pattern, leave the first layer of paint to dry thoroughly first. If you wish to print the other side of your bag, you must make sure that the first side is completely dry and fixed with an iron (step 8) before starting to print again.

11 When you have finished printing and your paint has dried, fix with a hot iron (follow the instructions for Wheels).

7. Foam Printing Blocks

Materials
Self-adhesive craft foam

Block printing ink or ink pads
Etching needle or sharp tool
Paper towel
Newspaper or scrap paper
Paper
Pencil
Printing tray
Roller
Ruler
Small scissors
Tracing paper
Transparent acrylic stamp blocks
  or firm plastic sheet

Tip
Larger pieces of foam can be printed without mounting onto blocks but a stiff background makes it easier to apply even pressure to your print.

Craft foam is great for making your own printing blocks. You can purchase precut shapes or cut out your own designs from craft foam sheets. In order to apply even pressure to your print and to be able to use a number of different things in your design, they need to be mounted on a stiff surface. Transparent acrylic stamp blocks allow you to see through your printing block to your printing surface. This makes them ideal, as it helps you see where you are aligning your patterns and colors and be much more accurate. If you aren't able to get hold of any, a piece of transparent firm plastic, from a folder or firm plastic container for example, is a good substitute.

1 Draw your design on the back of the self-adhesive foam or copy and trace the design templates (see page 76). Non-sticky craft foam is also suitable to use, but you will need to use double-sided tape or glue to stick the pieces to your acrylic. Cut out your shapes with a small pair of scissors.

2 Peel away the paper backing (or glue the back if not sticky) and stick your foam down onto your acrylic block, keeping each color of your pattern on a separate block.

4 Add details with an etching needle or sharp tool (like a pencil or an awl). Your marks will show through to the paper color background, since they don't pick up ink. For the cacti I've used different marks to make them look like different species.

5 You can be strict in the way you print your blocks in lines, print them across your paper randomly, or create a scene. Line up your different colors by looking through the block to arrange them in the positions you like best.
Ink your blocks, recoating each time you print.

3 Where you want colors to line up (like the pots), ink your first block and print onto the back of a sheet of foam. **A** Once dry, the ink provides a guide for drawing and cutting out your next pieces. Tape your second block to the first to prevent movement while you stick the pieces for your second color in position. **B**

Block-Printing Ink: Add a small amount of ink to your printing tray and roll out until your roller is evenly coated, then apply to your block very lightly. **A** If you are using an ink pad instead of a roller, stamp directly onto the block until evenly coated. **B**

Tip
Try to avoid getting ink on the back and sides of the block. Depending on the amount of pressure you apply when printing, this can transfer when you make a print. The flimsier plastic picks up the ink more readily, so wipe away any excess ink with a paper towel.

8. Printing with Flowers, Leaves, and Feathers

Cushion Covers

Beautiful detail, such as leaf veins, can be revealed by printing with natural objects. These bright cushions will bring nature inside your home and are sure to liven up your room or would make fantastic gifts.

1 Wash and dry the cushion covers to make sure that they are clean and have no trace of chemicals on them that could affect the printing. Once dry, iron them to get rid of all the creases (ask an adult to help if you are not confident with ironing). Insert a couple of flat sheets of newspaper inside the cushion as a barrier to prevent your paint from seeping through onto the back of the fabric.

Tips

- Choose a flat, close-weave fabric (ideally cotton) for your cushion covers. Think about what you will be printing, particularly the color and pattern. This will avoid costly mistakes.
- Pick flowers that are plentiful. Pick a few but leave the majority for the insects and others to enjoy.
- Avoid delicate or bulky flowers.
- Don't pick flowers from parks, community gardens, or nature reserves.
- If you don't have a garden, ask your neighbors if they will allow you to pick some of their flowers or leaves. Fall is a good time to find lots of differently shaped leaves that you can't usually reach.

2 Pick a selection of interestingly shaped flowers, leaves, and feathers. The flowers and leaves need to be robust enough to withstand printing and be reasonably flat. Pick the flowers and leaves you intend to print with in small batches, since they can wilt quickly, or pick them with their stems and place them in a container of water. The feathers should also be washed and dried before you start printing with them. I like the look of ruffled feathers; this can be achieved by gently teasing the vane (side bits) of the feather apart with your fingers.

Materials

Selection of flowers, leaves, and feathers

Board or wooden block
  (I used a piece of picture
  frame backing)
Fabric magic pen
Fabric paint
Iron
Newspaper
Plain cushion covers
Printing tray
Roller
Ruler
Scrap paper

Ironing Tips

- When ironing, don't leave the iron sitting on the fabric. Keep the iron moving across your fabric. This prevents your fabric from scalding or burning.
- Never leave your iron unattended. Switch it off.
- Once you have finished, allow the iron to cool completely before packing it away.

Geum

Helianthus

Maple

Shaft

Vane

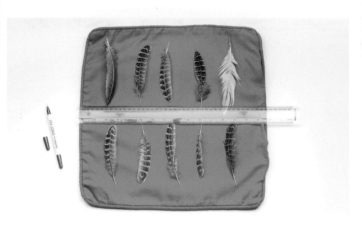

The leaf cushion has been printed with maple leaves, and the flower cushion with small helianthus (sunflower) and geum flower heads.

3 Lay out your design and, using a fabric pen and ruler, mark guidelines for your pattern. The magic pen marks vanish over time, but a fabric pencil or chalk, which won't leave a permanent mark and can be washed out once you have fixed your printing, could be used instead. Your guides can be small. I've used a cross to mark the position of the top and bottom of the feathers. The guides ensure that your objects can be placed back in the same position as you have laid out.

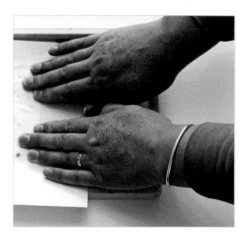

4 Paper spacers can be used to help you plan and mark out your design.

5 Mix your fabric paint in the printing tray and spread it out with a roller until you have an even coating. Place your flowers, leaves, or feathers onto the rolled paint.

6 Cover the printing tray with a piece of scrap paper, and press down gently over your object.

7 Gently lift off each item one by one. Check that they are fully coated with paint. If they're patchy, lay them back down onto the paint, and press gently again. Once they are fully coated they are ready to print with.

8 Use the guidelines that you have marked onto the cushion cover to place your painted object, *paint side down*, onto the fabric. Cover with a dry sheet of scrap paper and give the object a firm press (a board or wooden block on top of the paper may help you achieve the right amount of pressure). Because feathers are not totally flat, I ran my fingers along the center of the feather to make sure both sides printed evenly. Leaves and feathers can be recoated with paint and printed again, but you'll probably find that the flowers are not robust enough to go through the process of printing more than a couple of times, since they are so delicate.

Tip
• If a little paint gets where you don't want it, remove it by gently dabbing with a little soap on a damp cloth before the paint has dried or been fixed.

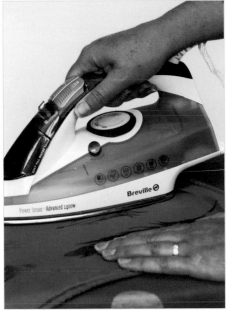

9 When you have printed the surface of the cushion, allow it to thoroughly dry. But keep the newspaper inside your cushion cover until the paint has fully dried all over.

10 Once dry, the paint needs to be fixed with a hot iron. Iron on a hot setting (cotton) for four to five minutes (or as instructions on your fabric paint bottle).

11 Fill your printed cushion cover with a cushion and enjoy.

9. Potato Printing

Materials
Potatoes

Paper for journal pages
Colored card for journal cover
Acrylic or block-printing ink
Binder clamps
Carving tools
Cookie cutter
Craft knife
Cutting mat
Eraser
Kitchen knife
Paper towel
Metal safety ruler
Paintbrush
Pencil
Printing tray
Scrap paper
Stapler

Journal Covers
Potatoes make great prints. They are quick and easy to carve and are a terrific way to gain confidence with using carving tools. You can print your potatoes randomly or choose to create repeat patterns.

For this project I've made journals that are 8.27 x 5.83 in. / 210 x 148 mm, but you could make any size you want; just remember that your cover will need to be slightly longer and wider than the paper inside. Instead of blank paper, you could bind together examples of your printing to record your progress, or you could stitch your journal together rather than using a stapler.

Opposite: For the cone of the ice cream I've used a slice of potato carved with cross-hatched lines, and for the chocolate flake I cut wavy lines. For the ice cream scoop, a slice from a small potato. The rabbit's body has been cut from the dashed lines, and the carrot from the straight lines. The hearts have been cut out using a cookie cutter from the slices carved with circles and straight lines.

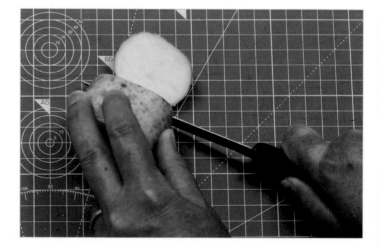

1 Cut your card to the size you need for your cover. It should to be slightly longer than your journal's page size, to extend over the edges of the paper when you fold the journal in half. If your card sheets aren't large enough, you will need to trim down your paper for the insides instead. Mark a guideline for the center with a pencil. This will show you where to staple.

Paper folded out flat

Colored card cut about 0.25 in. longer than the inside paper

2 Slice the potato into thick slices (at least 0.4 in. / 10 mm wide). Cut off the ends to stop the potato rocking, and provide a stable base while you carve. Then place the cut potatoes on a paper towel to absorb the watery juices that come out.

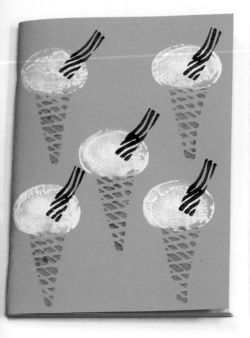

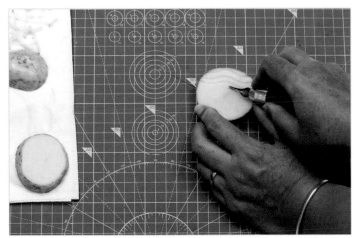

3 Carve different marks into the surface of each slice of potato (check out the examples on the next page). Keep your blade shallow, carve slowly to stay in control, and remember to keep your fingers well out of the way of the blade. When you have finished with each slice, keep it carved side down on a paper towel, since the potatoes will continue to ooze liquid.

4 Print with the potato slices as they are, or cut them down to the shape and size you require for your design, using, for example, a cookie cutter or a kitchen knife.

Carving

> ### Tips
> - These carving tools are sharp, so make extra sure that when you are carving you **cut away** from your body and keep your fingers well away from the direction of the blade.
> - If you make a mistake, just start again on the opposite side of your potato slice.
> - The larger your blade, the wider your carved lines or holes will be.

Straight lines: Starting from the edge of the potato nearest you, carve straight lines across the potato, cutting away from yourself. When you near your supporting hand, rotate the potato so that you keep your hand away from the carving tool. Try to keep the distance between your lines even.

Wavy lines: Weave your hand from side to side, like a snake, as you carve forward.

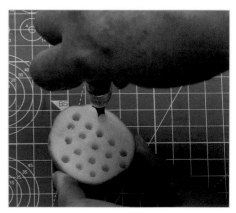

Cross-hatch: Repeat the straight lines. Rotate your potato and carve straight lines in the opposite direction.

Dashes: Start as if you were cutting a straight line. Keep your line short and angle your blade upward to flick the short line out.

Circles: Hold your carving tool straight above the potato and rotate in a full circle (as if you are drilling). Remove the circle by gently angling the blade upward. This will slice through the bottom, and the circular plug should pop out!

5 Mix your paint together thoroughly. Choose a paintbrush with a big head, then use it to coat the potato lightly with a layer of paint.

It needs to be applied lightly in order to prevent your carved lines from clogging up with paint and losing detail. If your carving does become clogged or your paint watery, remove the paint by printing onto a paper towel and then apply a thinner fresh coat of paint to your carving.

Eraser barrier

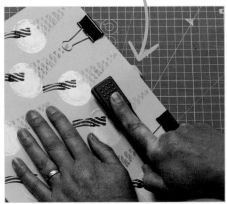

6 If you want to print a repeat pattern, you need to plan your design. Using a pencil, lightly mark the position of each repeat with a small cross. This will help you get your printing in the middle of the front and back covers and get your design straight. Allow the paint to dry between each color.

7 Lay the cover on top of your paper and hold them together with a couple of binder clamps. This prevents the paper from moving while you are binding. Lightly mark with a pencil 1.9 in. (5 cm) from the top and bottom of the center of your journal (along the spine); this will show you where to staple.

8 Open the stapler up and staple through your journal into an eraser, or similar barrier. Pull the eraser away and flatten the ends of the staple to close them. Remove any pencil marks and fold your journal in half. Weight it down with a heavy book overnight. It's then ready to fill with your designs.

10. Eraser Printing

Materials
Plain fabric pencil case

Card covered in newspaper
Carving tools
Erasers
Fabric ink pads
Fabric magic pen
Iron
Masking tape
Pencil
Ruler
Tracing paper

Tips
- If you want a small design, carve this out of a larger eraser and cut down to size once you have finished carving.
- You can print the star design in two different colors by inking either side of the eraser in different colors.

Pencil Cases

Rubber carving blocks are available for making stamps. But I'm sure you will have lots of spare erasers that are just perfect to recycle for this project!

A handprinted pencil case is ideal for keeping all your printmaking tools together, as well as for showcasing your creative and printmaking skills. Once you've finished printing with your eraser, it can be cleaned and used again to print another project—such as wrapping paper.

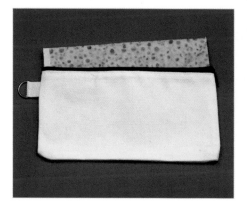

1 Insert into the pencil case a piece of cardboard, cut to the size of the case and covered with a sheet of newspaper. This works as a barrier to prevent your paint from seeping through onto the back of the fabric. The card also stretches the fabric and keeps it crease-free. If your zip won't allow your card to sit flat, just use the newspaper on its own.

2 Choose chunky erasers for carving, since very small erasers can be fiddly. You need to be able to hold your eraser safely so that your fingers are away from the carving tool, and provide enough room to control your carving to avoid slips or cause an injury.

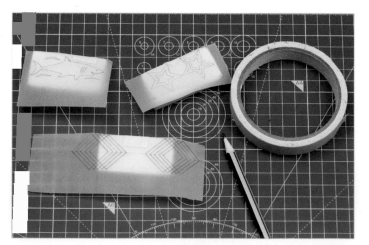

3 Using the templates on page 74, transfer your design onto your eraser. My erasers are 2.9 x 1.2 in. (59 x 30 mm), so if you are tracing them, that's what you need. You can make them bigger or smaller to fit your eraser if they are a different size. A piece of masking tape helps hold your tracing paper in place while you work. The eraser picks up the pencil marks really easily, so you should be able to rub over the design with your finger to transfer it rather than tracing. If necessary, use a pencil to go over your transferred design to make any faint lines clearer.

The star and shark designs have been printed as a brick repeat pattern, and the overlapping squares as regular tiling.

Follow the pattern instruction you wish to make, using steps 4 and 5.

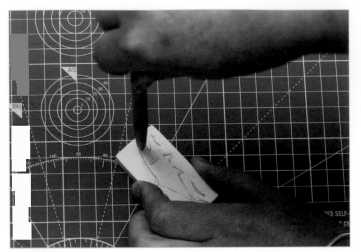

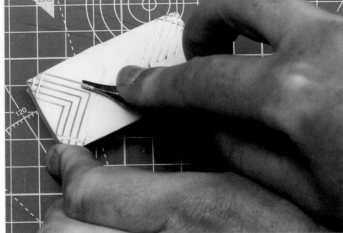

Shark

4 **a** Start with your finest blade and carve around the outline of the shark. You can then use a larger blade to remove the areas around the shark. Carve from the shark to the outside of the eraser, so if the blade slips, your shark will not be ruined.

5 **a** For the eye, use a sharp tool like an etching needle or a compass and wiggle it to make the hole bigger. Because rubber stretches, it makes it difficult to carve small, neat circles as you can with lino or potatoes.

Overlapping Squares

4 **b** Use a ruler to draw out the squares. Include the dashed guide lines on your tracing, since this helps you line the design up on the eraser in the middle. The equally spaced squares make a repeating pattern, so it's important to keep the distance between the lines even and that each end of your eraser is a mirror repeat. Line up the center of the squares on either end of your eraser to ensure this.

5 **b** Use your finest blade and carve a straight line from the center to the edge, then rotate your eraser and carve the opposite side. Repeat carving and rotating in this way to create each square.

Tips
- The cutting tools are sharp, so make sure that when you are cutting, you **cut away** from your body and **keep your fingers away** from the direction of the blade.
- Keep your blade angle shallow and carve slowly to stay in control!
- If you make a mistake, use the opposite side of your eraser to try again.
- Use an ink pad and a scrap piece of paper to check your carving. This will help show you if any areas still need to be removed.
- Mark the center on the back of your eraser, and mark which side is the top—see the photo to the right. This is really helpful, especially if you are distracted or when printing a brick repeat pattern.

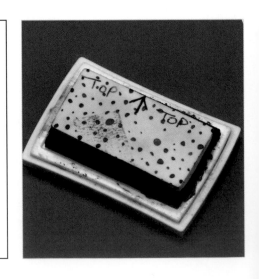

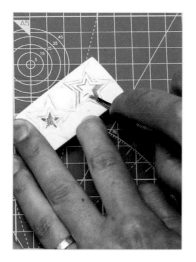

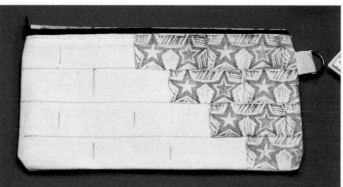

Stars

4 C Start with your finest blade and carve around the outline of the stars. To achieve crisp points, start from the pointy ends and carve away.

5 C Use a larger blade to remove the areas around the stars, working from the star to the outside of the eraser.

6 Place your eraser onto a sheet of newspaper and stamp the ink pad onto it until it is evenly coated. Print your pattern on a sheet of scrap paper; take your time to ensure that you line up your design.

7 Mark the center of your pencil case with a fabric magic pen and use the printed paper sample to line up your design. This ensures that your design will be central on the pencil case. Mark any additional guides as necessary with your fabric pen onto the pencil case to help you align your pattern.

8 Ink the eraser after each tile and print your design onto your pencil case. Once dry, the ink needs to be fixed with a hot iron. Iron on a hot setting (cotton) for around four to five minutes.

9 Remove the paper from the inside of the pencil case and fill with your favorite pens, printing tools, or other small items.

11. Lino Cards

Materials
Card

Baren or wooden spoon
Block-printing ink
Board or stiff cardboard
Carving tools
Lino
Masking tape
Newspaper
Pencil
Printing tray
Roller
Ruler
Tracing paper

I love getting cards—especially handmade ones. Lino is a perfect choice to use to print your own cards because it's quite tough and lasts a long time, which makes it ideal for invitations, festivities, or holidays, when you are making and sending out lots of cards.

Once you've carved your design, you can make it look different just by changing the color of the ink or the printing surface. You can print this ornament design in one color and then change it by using colored and textured card or paper. Or try coloring in your prints with paints or pens once they are dry. If you're feeling confident, you can register your design and print in more than one color. I have created two alternative designs for you to experiment with—you can find the templates on page 77. These are created in exactly the same way as the step-by-step procedure. Have fun and design your own patterns.

Tips
- If you have a large piece of lino, you will need to trim it down to size. This can take a number of strokes with a craft knife to cut all the way through. Traditional lino requires quite a lot of pressure, so I recommend you ask an adult for help with this.
- If your blade does slip while you are carving or you carve too far into your design, try to use the mistake in your design rather than throwing away the lino.
- With traditional lino, small amounts of debris and fine burlap hairs can pick up ink and transfer to your final print. To stop this from happening, once you are happy with your carving, make certain that you trim the edges neatly to remove any stay bits of burlap backing or curls of lino.
- Clean away all the debris from your work surface and lino to avoid picking debris up onto your print.

1 Copy the template on page 77 and transfer your design onto the lino with a pencil and tracing paper. Use a piece of masking tape to keep your tracing in place as you work. If you want to use a compass to draw the circle, the blue cross on the template marks the center. Go over your outline to make your lines clearer with a pencil or a permanent marker. Let all your pen marks dry properly, to avoid smudging.

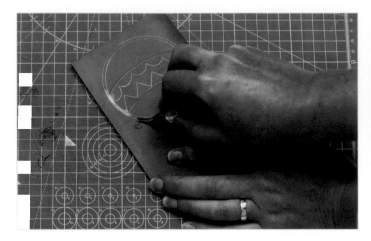

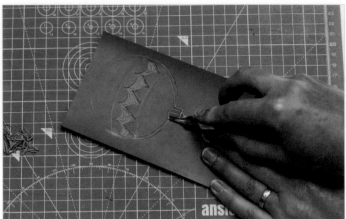

2 Start with your smallest blade and carve a key line (that's the outline) around the outside of your design. Don't rush. You need to be slow and steady to stay in control and prevent your blade from slipping. Keep the angle of your blade shallow and be careful that your hands and fingers are well away from the direction in which you are carving. Rotate your lino as you carve so that you can always carve away from your body.

3 Use the larger blades to remove areas where you don't want any ink, such as the background. Try to carve away from your design, to avoid carving too far into your design by accident. Some of the areas that you carve away will leave a trace. You can remove them completely or take advantage of them in your design by carving in the direction that complements your design (for example, I've carved vertical lines on the metal cap of the ornament).

4 Continue carving until you have removed all the areas where you don't want ink. Then add in details such as circles or fine lines.

5 Clean your work surface of any bits and pieces and put down some newspaper or scrap paper for inking. Roll out some ink in your printing tray with the roller, and work it in all directions over your lino to get an even coating.

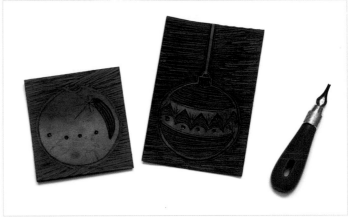

6 Print onto some scrap paper and use this to see if any areas on your lino need to be removed or tidied up. Once you are happy with it, you can use your carving to create a template to register your card and lino (see page 12), and to transfer the design onto a second piece of lino for a second color. Remember to draw guidelines for each piece of lino so you can place them back in exactly the same position.

7 Once the transfered ink is dry on your second piece of lino, draw on your design for the second color and carve away the areas where you don't want ink. The transfer helps make sure that your two colors line up. For my second piece of lino, I've carved away the background to leave the ornament shape and taken away areas where I want highlights (these show through to the color of the card you print on).

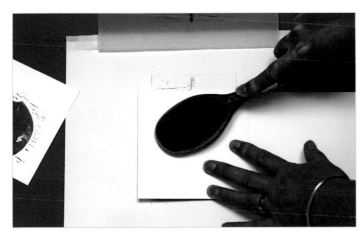

8 Use your guidelines to lay the lino and card back in the same position every time you print. Lay your card on top of the inked lino and use a baren or the back of a wooden spoon to rub over your block and make your print. If you find there is a lot of movement, you can fix your lino in position by using a piece of masking tape folded over on itself underneath the lino.

9 Print your ornament color first, followed by overprinting the outline. Allow each layer of ink to dry before printing the next. Wash and dry your lino, ink tray, and roller between different colors. wlf the ink is stubbornly stuck in the grooves of your lino, you can gently clean it with an old toothbrush or soft nail brush.

12. Lino Wrapping Paper

Now that you've created all these great gifts, you will need something to wrap them with! Any pattern can be used to print across a large area. You can print randomly or be stricter with the way you line them up. This takes concentration and accuracy, as well as some preparation, but the results once you have mastered them are sure to amaze everyone, and they provide great practice before you try printing on fabric or expensive specialty papers.

This project shows you a couple of alternative ways to take your patterns a stage further in order to help you cover larger areas.

Materials
Roll of paper or large sheet of paper

Block-printing ink
Carving tools
Cutting mat
Lino
Masking tape
Newspaper
Pencil
Printing tray
Roller
Ruler
Tracing paper

Interlocking Pattern

This pattern is created by overlapping a brick repeat. There is no flower on the right as this stem will share the smaller flower on the right when the pattern overlaps.

1 Transfer the flower design centered onto a piece of lino that is 6 in. / 15 cm in height, and carve.

2 Draw a grid 2 by 2 in. (5 by 5 cm) across your paper, using light pencil marks. The guides on a cutting mat will help you keep your lines horizontal and vertical. This grid helps you align your pattern. Any visible pencil marks can be removed with an eraser once you have finished printing and your ink is completely dry (you may find that they are covered by your ink and don't show).

3 Ink your lino. Keep your rolled ink thin and apply using light pressure. Rolling in all directions will help ensure your lino is evenly coated. You will need to recoat for every print that you make, which is tedious, but you will soon find that you pick up speed as you establish a rhythm. If your lino starts to clog with ink, wash clean with warm water and dry. A gentle scrub with a toothbrush or nail brush can help remove any stubborn ink.

4 Print the first column directly underneath one another (three squares down each time: 6 in. / 15 cm). For the next column, start your first print one square up and across from your previous column and then continue printing the remaining length of the column as before, directly underneath one another. Continue this pattern until your paper is covered.

Straight Repeat

1 Draw around your lino onto a piece of paper and cut out. Measure and draw equal quarters with a pencil, or fold in half horizontally and vertically. Number each quarter as above.

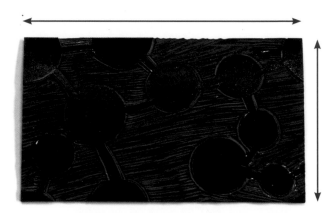

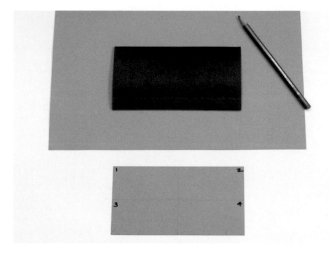

Tips

- If you are carving a tricky space where your design is on either side, carve to the middle of the space, stop, rotate your lino, and cut to your carving from the other side. This will avoid accidentally carving into the areas where you want ink.
- If your paper doesn't sit flat, weigh down the corners with something small but heavy (a jar, for example), or use masking tape either on the corners or folded over on itself underneath.

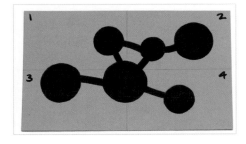

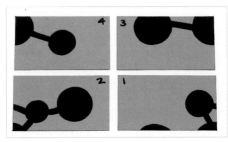

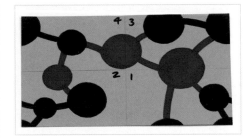

2 Draw the first part of the pattern in the center of your paper, making sure that the design doesn't touch or go over the edges.

3 Use the guides to cut your template in four, and rearrange the pieces as above (so the top is at the bottom and the left is on the right). Use masking tape on the back to stick your template back together.

4 Fill the central space with more of your design. This is where you can join your pattern together.

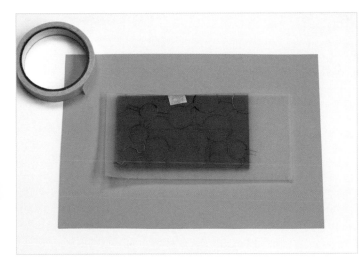

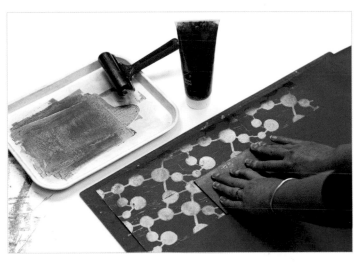

5 Copy your design onto tracing paper with a pencil and transfer onto the lino. Be careful to draw and carve the lines at the edges as accurately as possible, since this is where your design needs to line up and where any mistakes will show.

6 Print the pattern as a straight repeat. Use a straightedge of paper to line up your first print, and use the end of your print or lino to align your next print. Alternatively, measure the width and height of your lino and mark light horizontal and vertical guides (up and down guides) with a pencil across your paper to help alignment.

↑	↑	↑	↑
↑	↑	↑	↑
↑	↑	↑	↑

13. Relief-Printed Kite

Materials
Plain kite—I used a fish shape

Block-printing or acrylic paint
Clothespins
Craft knife or scissors
Cutting mat
Masking tape (thin and regular)
Materials for printing blocks:
  elastic bands, string, washers
Metal safety ruler
Paintbrush (for glue)
Paper for creating stencils
Pencil
Permanent black pen
Plant label
Plastic knife
Printing tray
PVA glue
Roller
Stiff cardboard
Tracing paper

Printing Blocks for the Kite:
Elastic bands in a chevron pattern,
a square of burlap, strips of string,
wooden pegs stuck to a block, half
a clothespin on its side, bottle top,
washer, dowel, plastic plant label,
and a plastic knife

Red kites, the birds, are regularly spotted flying overhead where I live, so what better inspiration for this kite!

These patterns have been made by using objects found around the home; a plastic knife, a plant label, elastic bands, string, a plastic bottle top, a washer, and a dowel. These have been used in combination with stencils and masking tape. You'll need a little patience, since there is some preparation before you can begin printing, and there is drying time for each layer of paint, but it's worth the wait to see this stunning kite fly.

Tips
• Make a selection of blocks and try printing with them on scrap paper first, before printing onto your kite.
• Print your kite in bright, bold colors (this isn't the project for subtlety). Your kite will be high in the sky, so it needs to be seen from a distance.
• Create a different bird design by altering the beak and head shape, changing the colors, or both.
• Use this simple equation to make your pattern bigger or smaller:

$$\frac{\text{Size you want}}{\text{Size you have}} \times 100 = \text{Your enlargement/reduction percentage}$$

---

1 Cut your cardboard into block-sized pieces (but not too large). If your cardboard is flimsy, glue a couple of pieces together to make them stiffer. Paint a generous layer of glue onto the cardboard, and stick down your objects. Leave the blocks to dry completely before printing with them.

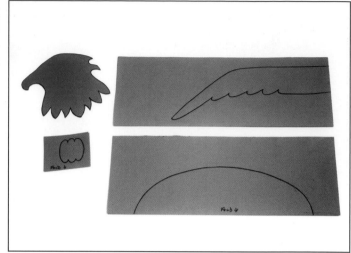

2 Stretch out your kite. Keeping it as taut and crease-free as possible, tape it down onto your work surface with masking tape. Your design will need to be printed onto the side with the central fin (in other words, the side that will face the ground when you take it outside to fly).

3 Copy the kite template on page 78, enlarge it to fit your kite (mine was enlarged by 200%), and trace the design onto both your kite and the stencil paper. I folded a sheet of paper in half and drew half the body on the fold line and the wings on the edge of the paper; this made it easier to cut out both the positive (the bird shape) and negative (the areas around the bird) stencils from a single sheet, since you will need both.

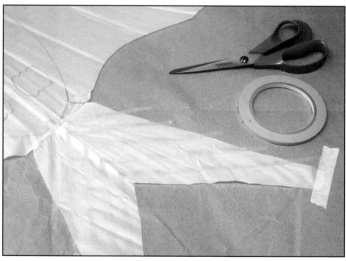

4 Using thin masking tape, mask diagonal stripes along the length of the tail. Run your finger along the length of each strip of tape to make certain that they have stuck to your kite all the way along.

5 **Red:** Use the positive body stencil to protect the body from any paint. Paint the tail and top of the wings in red paint. You could print these areas in the same way as the body, or with a sponge or a scrunched-up rag.

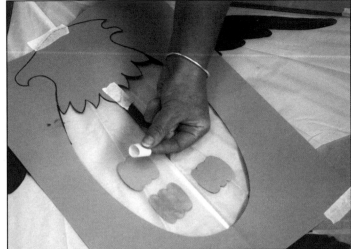

6 **Yellow:** Remove the body stencil and put it to one side for later use. Paint the beak and feet with yellow paint. Print the eye with a bottle top. Allow the paint to dry completely before moving on.

7 **Orange:** Use the negative stencil of the body and mask the top with a positive stencil of the head. Mask the feet. To keep them in position, fold a piece of masking tape over on itself to create a double-sided piece of tape. Print the body with a textured block. Lay your block on a sheet of newspaper, and roller the paint out over your block. I made a block by using a square of burlap.

Tips
*   Roll the central kite fin into a tight roll, and mask it to keep out of the way of your printing (you may have to work around it, printing one side and then the other).
*   It's boring waiting for paint to dry, but it's important that you don't rush ahead, since your paint can easily end up smudging and become ruined. Avoid thick paint, which will take much longer to dry. You can help reduce the drying time with a hair dryer if you're really impatient!
*   A damp cotton swab can be used to remove any paint that manages to get in the wrong place, or to clean up any paint that may have seeped underneath your masking tape.

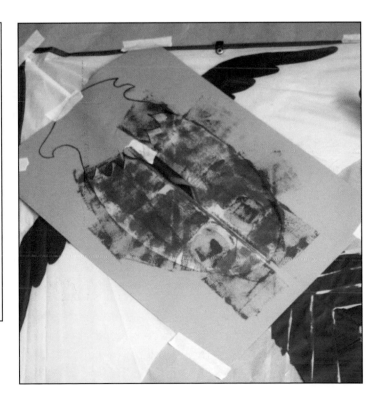

8 **Black:** Overprint your orange paint with a block that will make it look like feather highlights. I've used a block made with strips of string.

9 **Black:** Remove the stencils and overprint your yellow eye with the washer. Add the pupil and nostril details. I used a wooden dowel for this, but any small, circular object such as the end of a pencil would be suitable. Allow your paint to dry.

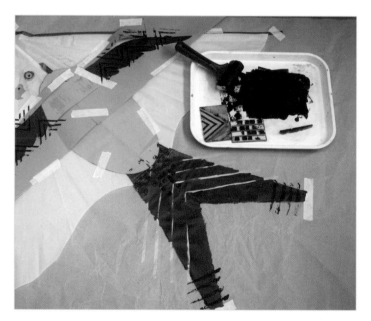

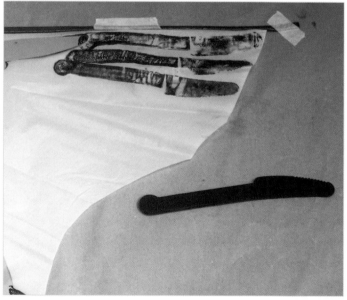

10 **Black:** Replace the stencils with the positive body and the negative wings. Add patterns to the top of the wings and tail. I've used a chevron made from elastic bands along the top of the wing, a block made from wooden clothespins at the top of the tail, and a pin on its side for the stripes on the tips of the tail.

11 **Black:** Work from the bottom of the kite up to the top of the wings to create a layered effect for the feathers. Print three feathers on each side in black, using a plastic knife.

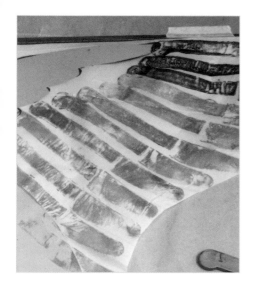

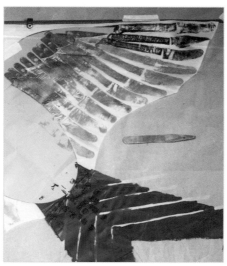

12 **Gray:** Wash and dry your knife and then continue to fill the rest of the row in with printed gray knives.

13 **Metallic bronze:** With a plastic plant label follow the line of the top wing and overprint the next row of feathers in a metallic bronze paint.

14 **Brown:** For the top row, I used the opposite end of the plant label printed in dark brown. Allow your paint to dry thoroughly.

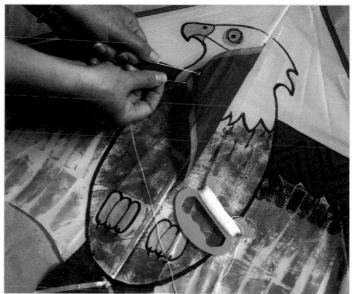

15 Remove all the masking tape and stencils. Use a thick, black, permanent pen to outline your kite and give your Red Kite definition.

16 Tie the string to the fin and fit the tension bar to the back. Choose a clear, open space with no overhead wires or branches, wait for some wind, and launch your Red Kite.

14. Screen-Printed T-shirt

Materials
Plain T-shirt

Cutting mat
Fine misting bottle filled with
 water, plus a cloth
Paper or stencil board
Pencil
Scissors or craft knife
Scrap paper
Screen-printing frame
Screen-printing tape or
packaging tape
Spoon or palette knife
Squeegee
Stiff cardboard + newspaper
Textile-screen-printing ink
Tracing paper
Iron

Tips
- Test your printing onto a similar-colored piece of paper (or scrap fabric) before printing on your final garment, to be confident that your print will look exactly the way you want.
- A printing tray kept close by is really handy to put your squeegee or spoon on. This will help keep your work surface clean.

Screen printing produces sharp and crisp lines, which makes it perfect for transferring designs onto garments or fabric. Once you've created your stencil, you can keep pulling (the technical term for making) prints until either your stencil paper deteriorates or you want to change color. This way you can create more than one T-shirt or print on different garments or surfaces. This is absolutely great if you are creating a design or emblem for a team or group, but it also works well if you want to design your own clothes with your own unique logo!

1 Wash, dry, and iron your T-shirt to ensure that it is clean and crease-free (yes, boring, but essential to avoid ruining your T-shirt). Insert a sheet of newspaper inside the T-shirt as a barrier to prevent the ink from seeping through onto the other side of the fabric. Also, if you have a piece of card or board, you can insert this underneath the newspaper to help stretch the T-shirt and keep it crease-free—this makes it much easier to print on.

2 Photocopy the template on page 80, enlarging it by 200%, or draw your own design onto your stencil paper.

3 Use a small pair of scissors or a craft knife to cut out your design. The paper masks where you don't want ink, and the holes allow the ink to transfer to your garment. If you are using scissors, pinch the paper together and snip into the area to be removed to create a cut. This allows you to insert your scissors and maneuver cutting without breaking the outside edge of your stencil.

4 Lay your stencil underneath the screen, keeping a larger area free at the top for the ink. As you look through the screen, your stencil should look the way you want it to print. Mist your screen with water and wipe with a cloth to remove any excess. This dampens your screen, which helps prevent the ink from clogging and sticks your stencil to the underside of the screen, ready to print.

Tip
Mark the position of your sample paper or mask a piece of tracing paper onto the board underneath the screen and print onto the tracing paper. This will help you line up your design. This is really handy if you are printing more than one T-shirt or color, but not essential if you are printing just one.

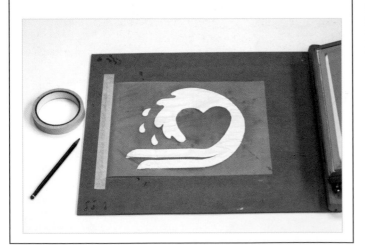

5 Use screen or packaging tape to mask the inside of your frame where any gaps show around your stencil--where you don't want any ink. Mask a larger area at the top of the screen (a couple of widths of tape) so that you can spread out your ink without transferring it onto the printing surface.

6 Spoon a line of textile-screen-printing ink along the top of the screen.

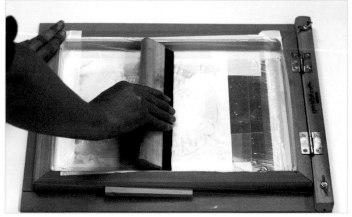

7 Use one hand to keep the screen steady, and the other to pull the ink evenly and firmly across the screen with your squeegee. Use your squeegee to lift the remaining ink up and return it to the top of the screen. You will need to pull the ink across the screen a couple of times to make a good print.

8 Print your T-shirt in the same way. Ensure that you are happy with the position of your T-shirt before laying the screen down over the top and pulling your print. You can use your sample or tracing paper to help position the T-shirt in the right place. Remove your T-shirt and put it somewhere safe to dry, but don't remove the newspaper or card until the ink is completely dry.

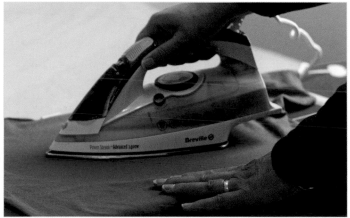

9 Turn your T-shirt inside out and iron on the back of the design on a hot setting for two minutes (or follow the instructions on your textile-screen-printing ink) to fix your print.

15. Screen-Printed Poster

Materials
Paper

Drawing fluid
Fine paintbrush
Masking tape
Nail brush
Old toothbrush
Pencil
Scrap paper
Screen block
Screen-printing frame
Screen-printing tape or packaging tape
Screen-printing ink
Spoon or palette knife
Squeegee
Screen cleaning fluid

Whether you need to deliver information or want a decorative poster for your wall, this method of screen printing allows you to create more-complex designs than paper templates do.

Allow yourself plenty of time for this project, since there is lots of drying time while setting up, but the printing part is quick! You will find a drying rack really helpful. It's worth setting this up before you start printing, to prevent your prints from being damaged while drying (see page 15).

1 Using the template on page 79, draw the outline of your design directly onto the screen with a soft pencil: start with the background (orange), followed by overprinting the zebra stripes (black). You can use masking tape to fix the template underneath your screen and trace the design onto the inside of the screen.

Tips
- Drawing fluid can be washed out if you make a mistake, or touched up with a damp cotton swab in small areas.
- Cut all your paper down to the same size, to make absolutely certain that all your posters are registered in the same position.

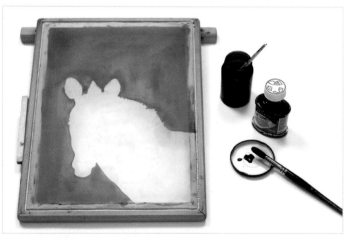

2 Turn your screen over to paint on its back (the screen needs to be slightly elevated to prevent the screen from touching the surface). Shake the bottle of drawing fluid well before opening, and paint your design onto the screen as a positive image (your design should appear as you want it to print, as you look through your screen as if printing). You need to soak the mesh with the fluid, without it being overly thick or bubbling.

3 Keep your screen flat but elevated from your work surface, while the drawing fluid dries.

4 Place some scrap paper underneath the screen. Lift the screen slightly to stop the mesh touching the surface—I used a couple of blocks of wood for this. Squeeze a line of screen block at the top of the screen, then pull your squeegee evenly across the screen.

5 Keep the screen slightly lifted up to dry (this takes about an hour). Once it's completely dry, set the screen in a sink, preferably with running water. Use an old toothbrush or similar tool and, using the water, remove the drawing fluid by scrubbing gently in small circles. Allow the screen to dry once all the drawing fluid has been removed—on top of a radiator or somewhere warm—outside if it is sunny!

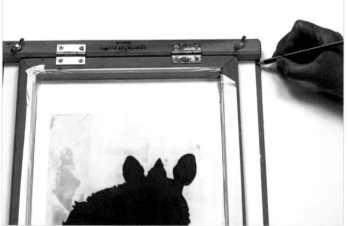

6 Mask the sides of the screen with tape. The screen needs to be completely dry, since the tape will not fix securely to the screen if it is still damp. Make sure the tape is fixed securely to the screen, since any gaps will allow ink to seep underneath and likely ruin the print.

7 Mark the position of your printing paper on the backing board (or the corners of the screen onto your paper if your frame is not fixed to a board), so that you can position it back in the same position for subsequent color layers.

8 Spoon a bead of ink across the top of the screen and pull down the screen with your squeegee (you may need to repeat the pull to achieve a good coat of ink). Place a hand on your paper to avoid movement as you lift up the screen.

Clip your print onto the drying rack, and print another. Print more posters than you need, to allow for errors. For variety, you could wash and dry your screen and print the background in a different color.

9 Once you are happy that you have printed enough of your first color, remove the design from the screen with screen-printing cleaning fluid. Apply the cleaning fluid to both the front and back of the screen and leave for a few minutes before scrubbing clean under running water with a nail brush (or toothbrush for awkward corners). Give your screen a final rinse with water and leave to dry.

10 Lay a dry print in position to help you align the zebra stripes, and repeat the same process following steps 1–9. You can print a multicolored zebra by spooning more than one color across the top of your screen.

Drypoint with Tetra Pak®

Eraser Printing—Pencil Cases

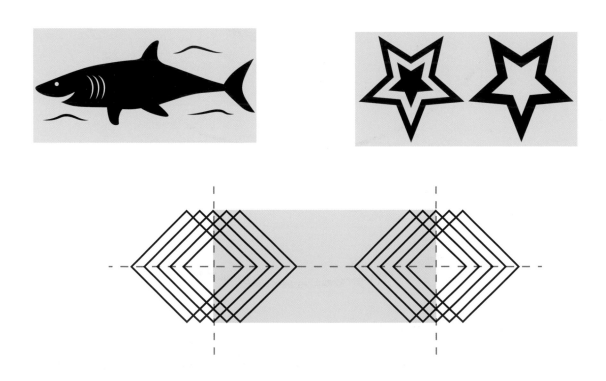

Cork Stamps and Decoder Disk

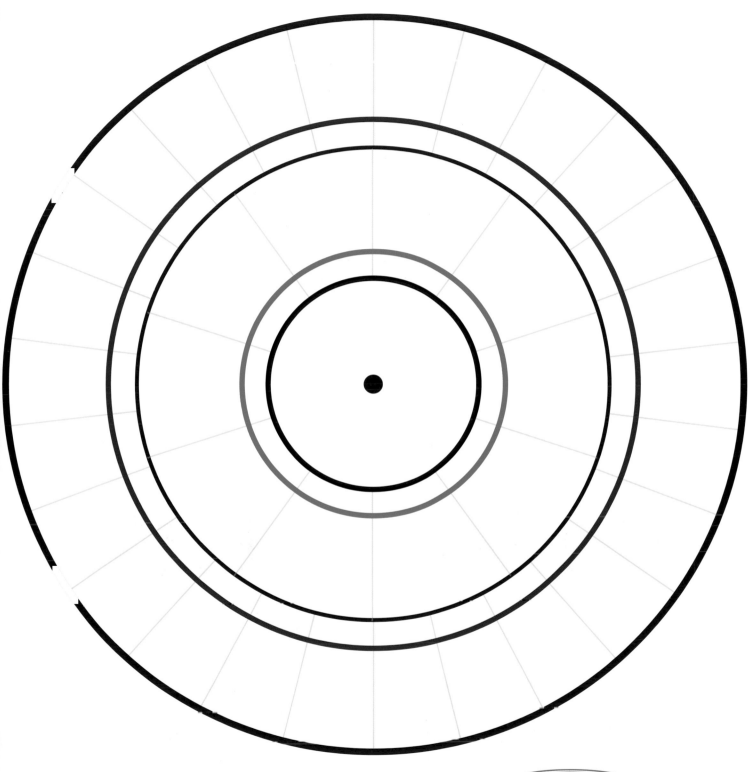

Here are the 3 parts of the decoder. Ensure that you copy these the same size as shown so that all your code elements will fit. The decoder is assembled as shown.

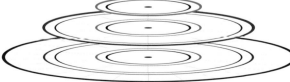

Foam Printing Blocks

Lino Wrapping Paper

Lino Cards

Relief-Printed Kite

Screen-Printed Poster

Bird Collage

Body

Back

Wing

Beak

Tail

Screen-Printed T-shirt